SCARS & STARS

ALSO BY JESSE THISTLE

From the Ashes

SCARS
&
STARS

Jesse Thistle

Illustrations by Karen McBride

McClelland & Stewart

LIBRARY AND ARCHIVES CANADA CATALOGUING IN PUBLICATION

Title: Scars and stars : poems / Jesse Thistle.
Names: Thistle, Jesse, author.
Identifiers: Canadiana (print) 20220195706 | Canadiana (ebook) 20220195714 |
ISBN 9780771003509 (hardcover) | ISBN 9780771003516 (EPUB)
Classification: LCC PS8639.H554 S33 2022 | DDC C811/.6—dc23

"Juneau" is from FROM THE ASHES: My Story of Being Indigenous,
Homeless, and Finding My Way by Jesse Thistle. Copyright © 2021 by Jesse
Thistle. Reprinted with the permission of Simon & Schuster Canada, a division
of Simon & Schuster, Inc. All rights reserved.

Book design by Emma Dolan
Jacket art: (stars) grebeshkovmaxim / iStock / Getty Images Plus;
(texture) studiocasper / iStock / Getty Images Plus
Interior art © Karen McBride
Typeset in Fournier MT Pro by M&S, Toronto
Printed in Canada

McClelland & Stewart,
a division of Penguin Random House Canada Limited,
a Penguin Random House Company
www.penguinrandomhouse.ca

1   2   3   4   5   26   25   24   23   22

Penguin
Random House
McCLELLAND & STEWART

I dedicate this book to anyone who is struggling
as I have done my whole life. I offer you a tool:
this book of poetry. I hand over to you my most
valuable gift. The one that saved me years ago.
The one I have hidden from the world until now
because I have been selfish. But it is not mine to hoard.
Never was. I just borrowed it until I was strong enough
to stand on my own—it is time to give it to another.
May it protect you as it has me. May it give you the
unconquerable heart of a god. And may it also make you
immortal, if only until you find safe harbour,
in your quest to find peace and love.

SCARLIGHT

Scars can be beautiful or ugly; it's just how you look at them.

They adorn our skin, tell us where we've been, and all
we've survived.

My most gruesome scar both destroyed and rebirthed me.

It's an Achilles tendon injury, from when I fell off a building
and shattered my right leg from the shin bone down.

Things really looked bad for me back then.

Crippled, addicted, homeless, too.

I had reconstructive surgery; my foot and heel are held
together by titanium wires and screws—bone on wire,
each and every step.

Doctors thought I'd need medical aid to walk again—but I showed them.

One day long ago, at the beginning of my genesis, and full of doubt, I decided that I wasn't going to lay down and die.

I decided to rob a store because, out on the streets and wandering, I felt I wasn't getting the healthcare that I needed to heal my now infected foot which was in danger of amputation.

It was a drastic and desperate move that forced the state to take care of me, and lucky for me it worked. I got to keep my leg after jail staff gave me proper food, rest, and antibiotics.

I started walking slowly in custody. I first limped from one railing to another. From the court bench to the holding cells and back again. My foot throbbed, but I was determined.

Then I hobbled, from one jail cell to the next, the range shower to my bunk and back again. The pain became more tolerable somewhat with each muster.

Next, I shuffled in a rehab facility, one step after another from one end of the compound to the other. Again, the jolts of leg-electricity were more manageable, strangely, the harder I worked my foot.

Running followed, and I fell flat on my face the first time
   I tried. But falling felt so good.

After a few more tumbles I worked myself up to a kilometre,
   then after that, three, then five.

In summer 2008, I ran a half-marathon every Friday for
   eight weeks straight and even attempted a full
   marathon, but fell on the thirty-third kilometre.

My foot just couldn't get the job done, held together by
   little more than willpower.

That was tough to accept—to admit I just didn't have it in me.

But a strange calm came over me as I struggled to my feet.
   I realized that everything was as it should be and that I'd
   taken thousands more steps than I thought I ever would.

Soon, my sponsor Randal, my buddy Burnt McBurnt, and
   the other guys at Harvest House came and carried me
   across the finish line. I didn't walk for three weeks after
   that marathon attempt.

In honour of my renaissance, my greatest gladiatorial struggle,
   I write about my scar, the deepest yet most beautiful one,
   the one that taught me to walk again, and the one that
   gave me the gift of poetry—a language of creation; a
   divine ambrosia; a balm for others with similar scars.

Sweetgrass

THE SHIELD OF ACHILLES

Anyone who really knows me will tell you I bear the mark of Achilles on my right ankle and heel. Years ago, I shattered my lower right leg bones in a drunken misjudgment of risk. I am lucky to walk today. If you've read my memoir, *From the Ashes*, you know the story. I limp pretty severely now, tilted to one side like Tamerlane the fourteenth-century Turco-Mongol conqueror, but that hasn't stopped me from losing sixty pounds these last two years of the pandemic. The pain is unreal, however, and I don't know how many more years I can hang on—you can only train the brain to accept so much, same with an ankle constructed with screws and wires—until it all gives way. I fear that day. I fear that pain. I fear what I will do when I finally give up. As a recovering addict, I can't use narcotics to numb it out like everyone else. All I can do is hang on until I can't. Poetry helps me do that.

People think that because I am a high-performing assistant professor and author that I am somehow okay. As if someone who's been undead and endured the underworld of Hades can ever be okay. As if someone whose leg is mangled can ever forget what it was to run fully mobile with the wind in their hair and without pain. Was Achilles okay after Paris shot his ankle? What became of him? Remember, he was half-god; I am but a mortal.

I think of the *Iliad* and *Odyssey* often, and it gives me permission to die and forever turn to ash and cross the River Styx as Achilles did. I feel this way when I can't handle life—*it would be acceptable to toss in the towel*, I figure, *and use the convict's braid* (you'll know what I am talking about when you read the poem); *no one should have to live with a throbbing leg like mine*. Sometimes, after the long country walks I've taken these last twelve years, when my foot is pulsing and my wound's scar tissue has opened up down to the bone, I do what I always have done to stay sober from crack cocaine since 2008—I write poems. I try to get it out on paper. That takes my mind off shit.

I remembered hearing the story of Achilles years ago when I was homeless—I'd heard of him but didn't know the whole legend. The ancient warrior's physical woe, I learned, replicated itself in my plight—when you damage your Achilles tendon you're pretty much finished. I realized I probably wasn't going to walk on my own again—this was the time when I had a raging infection after a failed surgery and was staying in shelters and tripping around as the wind blew, the world as hopeless as *The Raft of the Medusa*. But I also heard how Achilles had this cool shield made by the god Hephaestus and that it had hammered into its golden face all of the ancient world's wonders—feasts, civilization, the polis, great battles, palaces, mountains, all the animals, Earth, Sun, the heavens and stars, vineyards, oceans, and everything else in existence. It had everything but poetry. Poetry, the legend said, was left out purposefully, for poetry had the power to make the world anew, to conjure up all of creation. Poetry was the shield itself.

The tale of Achilles' Shield protected and gave me great courage as I ventured through my life. It was an incredible tool of perception and agency and made me stop feeling sorry for myself and start seeing all the darkness and tragedy around me as beautiful, in a way, if that makes any sense. Everything was suddenly and completely part of this grand and spectacular project of poetry, the jagged edges of the world violently beaten into exquisite and terrible shapes, through life's forge of toil and suffering, but always to emphasize or better express some beauty, even in the grotesque and lost, even the vile, and even the festering wounds that formed into hideous scars, like my own.

I remember trying to see the good, then, even whilst gripping my imaginary buckler and robbing a store and being taken into custody. I remember thinking that even the intake guards strip searching me, making me grab my ankles and cough, was a kind of poetry. So was the look on the judge's face when he confronted me about my addiction behavior.

So, too, was the ash and water the inmates drove into their arms with illegal guitar strings and tattoo machines. So, too, were the holes my sex work friends ripped into their veins with needles filled with puddle water and heroin. So, too, was the horrid stench of my necrotic leg; the fear; the guns to my head; the total helplessness I had wandering the streets of Ottawa. All of it had a kind of dark beauty to it, like images— my images—hammered into my ethereal golden shield on my anvil of hardship and mental illness.

But as I collected my scars in the crafting of this book, I realized that great and significant beauty had also always lit my way. For how else would I see? How else could I admire or even see my scars but by the light of the stars; the light of those gentle and kind souls who'd been there amid the darkness and saved me thousands of times out there? They were and are my firmament, the stars and moon who navigated me to the safe harbour of my new life today—the street workers, my family, my times in the shelter, the rehab staff, the recovering addicts, my wife Lucie, the connection to Creator, the joy of fatherhood, my grandparents who took us in, my mother and father who'd tried their best, going to university and reconnecting with my maternal Métis-Cree heritage, and the wonderful neighbours and loved ones who surround me now and whose Tupperware containers fill my kitchen cupboard, offerings from when my daughter Rose was born. These are all living poetry; muses I catch like fireflies. They, too, had to be honoured.

And, so, with my net, I raked the heavens of my memory and stole down the celestial bodies and set them onto the pages before you, so you could also see the shadows and shapes and supernovas on my shield, the dark and light crevasses of my being, the gods and demons I know, the poetry of my life.

Tobacco Flowers

Part One

★

A PRIVATE WAR

Withdrawal. I could feel it coming. That unending ancient ache. That torment that screamed within my bones and made my flesh crawl. That uneasiness that made me incontinent and delirious. I vowed to increase my begging and be honest with every passerby; I needed their money to stave off the coming seizures.

God appreciates honesty.

The futility of begging wasn't lost on me, but I put my faith in it anyway.

The first guy down the road had slicked-back hair and a powder-grey suit. He was in a rush.

"Excuse me, sir. Do you have some change, I've—"

"Nah, man. Fuck off."

He was gone as soon as he appeared. Didn't even have a chance to tell him my dilemma.

People are busy. It's not his fault.

I brushed myself off for the next person, but she was gone faster than the last guy. She never even acknowledged my question.

"Busy, busy," I said under my breath. "People are busy."

I searched Rideau station for tossed cigarettes.

Bingo.

There was one near the McDonald's entrance behind the bus stop.

The rubbie, although repugnant, took my mind off dope sickness, if only for a second.

I'm transforming, I thought, dashing my ash with yellowed fingers, *into some kind of disheveled homeless wizard.*

Just then an OC Transport bus hurled onto the platform, loaded with a fresh batch of would-be donor-passengers. The side doors opened and people jousted with one another on their way to work.

I dove in to assert myself.

"Excuse me, I'm dope sick. I need change!"

My begging meant nothing to them; I was background noise on the way to the fridge for a commercial break.

"I said," with raised voice, "I'm sore. Please, help!"

Again, nothing, just vacant eyes and the backs of people's heads as they trailed off into Rideau Mall or up to Parliament Hill.

I bet they all have really important things to do, just like you used to . . .

My mind drifted back to my first job at Food City in the produce department. I worked the afterschool shift dressed to the nines in my black tie, crisp white shirt, and spotless white smock, my hair combed to perfection. All the ladies—young and old—used to ask me to pick their fruits and vegetables. They'd smile and bat their eyelashes and ask me questions they already knew the answers to. And they'd always giggle at my dry grocery-store humour: "*Orange* you glad to Vitamin C me?" Terrible, I know. But it was a good job that helped with my self-confidence.

In that bus station, fearing dope sickness, I remembered trimming the rust off the lettuce, stacking the apples in perfect pyramids. I missed being clean and proud with my spiffy hair. I missed being handsome and helping the lovely ladies to their produce. And I missed being busy like the people who now ignored me on their way to work.

*

Harmful memories like this one plague me constantly, even in my new life, safe and far off in my ivory tower or on stage among the literati. To be alone, afraid, and haunted by life leaves one hollow and isolated (as the above prose shows), but that is only if one doesn't step back and realize it's all part of the shield—even madness and filth, even heartbreak and chaos, or monumental loss like the loss of a leg, or a child, or lifelong suicidal ideation. I write about all of this in these poems, the violence of past wars I've endured beaten into metal, the multitude of sword and axe blows endured upon my shield, and their disfigured gouges and dents are expressions of my survivance; and that gives me deep appreciation today of how far I've journeyed, to see how far away begging in Rideau bus station really is. Some of the people I reference or write about explicitly have passed along to the spirit world; some of the places were bulldozed and paved over long ago. I mourn their loss with you, my reader. And I am glad that, if only for a second, you can see them as I do, as living poetry, eternal monuments in time, testaments to the terrible beauty of this world.

A PEACEFUL SUICIDE

I saw your pretty gun
and begged you
to shoot me right between the eyes.

I was sick of wandering, no place to go.
Sick of the addiction, sick of not having a face.
I told you I had $5,000, loot from a fresh score.
Said it'd be all yours
if you'd just fire a bouquet of roses through my forehead,
spray the cement wall.

You agreed and we went to the spot.
You pointed the barrel and paused
then started pistol-whipping me
as I fell to the ground.

"I knew you didn't have it," you said, pulling out a lousy
    twenty from my pockets. "Besides, you're not worth
    the bullet."

This memory haunts me some mornings, before my coffee
    and hugs.

A part of me still ashamed,
A part of me still wishing you pulled the trigger.

I awake in the bullpen
Arrested again, I figure.
Alcohol again, I know.

I blacked out yesterday
and now I'm all covered in blood
like I've killed someone.

Horrified,
I panic and search memory
trying to remember this horrific mark of Cain.

"You're in real trouble this time," a policewoman calls back.
"We found you in the street beating yourself up again."

My ancestors fall around me like spent cherry blossoms,
     jogging my memory
I see broken hands pummeling asphalt, my head clubbed
     through the bus station glass
I see blue and red lights, seven cops, and my arrest on the grass.

It is then that I realize, as I collapsed on the floor.
That I'm the lone bloody causality of my own private war.

FISH MARKET TRIUMPH

Years ago, the city was my tundra,
back when I wandered in unending winter nights
back when I was snow-blind from cocaine
back when shadows and insanity were my only companions.

The cold gnawed my bones then,
slowed my speech, tangled my legs
made each snowbank an inviting pillow
made each snowdrift a warm bed.

But, each morning, without fail, a shaft of dawn's light
    shone down triumphant
driving away the darkness and reminding me not to give in
and that I'd earned my spot in the sun;
my little panhandling spot near the fish market.

There
on the steps of the shelter
we met, both relapsing from rehab.
We knew this wasn't who we really were.
I turned my back to the cold,
searched for police
up the alley,
down the sidewalk
and street.

"It's no use, Jess," you said. "We're already caught by
     something much worse."
I nodded, glanced past you,
watched the city lights as they hummed
against the tracks
and stars
and all of our scars.

I wore a cheap suit when I was released from custody.
I slicked my hair, shined my shoes, pressed my shirts and
    pants, and tied my tie in a big Windsor knot like it was
    my religion.
Every time I left the house, I dressed like that.
That is, until my uncle told me to cool it on the suit.

You see, I was trying to show the world my worth with a
    tube of gel and a late-1990s ill-fitting donated suit. It
    was my way of proving I was worth a second chance.

Today on my way home on the bus I saw a guy like that.
He was fresh out of jail with a cheap suit on, just like I
    used to wear.
Rough around the edges,
prison tattoo peeking out of his collar,
eye sockets filling in from past addictions,
and his knuckles scarred from holding his ground inside.

In that moment, I turned my head and said a prayer for
    him and asked God to help him find his way.

Creator only knows how many prayers like this were
done for me back when I first learned to love
myself again.

THE CONVICT'S BRAID

I turn the braid in upon itself,
the outside turned
over
the last outside strands.
Again,
I pull and weave.
The outside, over the outside,
until it's tight, until it's one long beautiful braid.

Jail staff watch us; we are not allowed braids.
The COs, if they catch us, they take them.
Torn-up bedsheets,
braided into vehicles of escape,
nooses to hang ourselves with,
and tonight I'll try again.

Undercover cops could never figure out
how we could spot them
each and every time.

They'd come with clothes like ours
dirty and soiled
shoes falling apart.

They'd come knowing all the lingo
where to buy dope
who the players were.

They'd come knowing the pimps were just parasites,
and it was the ladies who really ran things
as they were the ones who carried the drugs between spots.

In many ways they were us
camouflaged all to hell
except they could never figure out how we knew.

You see, when they'd come to the trap house
the dealer would take them into a private room
and demand they take their shoes off and show them the
     bottom of their feet.

Why?

Because junkies and crackheads have feet
like marathon runners on an endless sojourn into chemical
    slavery
layers of callouses and broken toenails.

You can't fake that,
an addict's street-feet passport,
though the police did try.

You ever been hunted?
A bounty on your head?

And I'm not talking about someone coming to destroy your
    career or idea.
I'm talking about someone coming to physically execute you.

Well,
let me tell you:
there's nothing more terrifying
exhilarating
nothing that tests your intelligence more.

I was hunted, once, because I'd betrayed the "code"
I spoke my mind
I stood up—alone—against a senseless murder.

In the end, there was no protection
no recognition
no safety
all there was left was justice.
That, and misinformation and judgment from onlookers.

I realized pretty quick the high cost of justice

it is a lonely island

a banished existence

a dream held by idealists and fools; those out there among
the hunted.

The hardest part about being homeless was
not hearing my own name for months at a time.
The silence of identity.

I never told anyone my name,
for fear of reprisal, for being a "rat."
I drifted for years
between lives and cities and civilizations and shelters
always afraid to tell people my name.

Looking back, that was what hurt most—
not hearing my name.
Sometimes I'd wander alone,
and whisper *Jesse* just to hear it,
a reminder that I was still me,
and still human,
and that I, too, had a name.

Scottish bull thistle

Part Two

*

SHOW ME
YOUR SCARS

In 2018 I decided to go back home and see my old associates after almost ten years away. I wanted to get some inspiration for a few writing projects and figured there was no better place to mine prose than suburban Hades, my hometown of Brampton, so off I went.

When I got to our old headquarters on Main Street, I knocked on the thick steel door. The frame and brass handle were reinforced and beefy, security measures, just like back in the day. A deep voice barked from within, "Who dat!?" It sounded like my old friend Marco, but it was hard to tell behind two inches of peeling paint, metal, and reinforced concrete. A flash of light shone through the peephole. "Who is there!?" the voice queried once again, the light now gone.

"It's me, Jesse," I said, my face glued to the peephole. "It's Crackula . . . let me in . . ."

A shadow shifted in the foyer and there was the unmistakable tick of a revolver muzzle against the back of the steel door. I moved out of the line of fire just in case.

"Nah, guy!" the voice said. "Jesse's dead."

Only when I held my driver's licence up to the peephole did he really believe it was me. Fifty locks and chains unzipped and the door swung open faster than Usain Bolt. There he was, my old friend Marco, his hair greyer and belly rounder than I remembered, but he was still my old road dog.

"You crazy fucker, look at you, you've put on weight," he said as he shook my shoulders, choked up a little. "I heard you died years ago, hunted."

I did, I wanted to say, *a thousand times*—but nothing came out.

"Well," he exclaimed, arm around me now, "it's nice to see you breathing. There were so many rumors about you— one that you'd OD'd, lost your mind, one that you were killed." Marco broadcasted yesterday's gossip like an honest Walter Cronkite. "Last time I saw you," he said, "you were rail-thin and just out of custody. We all thought you'd OD in the first three days out like everyone else." I suddenly felt like a Native Jacob Marley, the ghost of drug-users past, visiting a Trinidadian Ebenezer Scrooge. I was also thankful I didn't OD upon release way back when.

A few of my old buddies heard us talking and came over. "Yeah, dog, you're supposed to be dead," my one buddy JD hollered as he pushed Marco aside and dropped a top-rope elbow on my face from the stairs, "but here you are—alive and well." I reciprocated the love with a death punch to the solar plexus and we all kind of just rolled around like adolescent wolves, not quite playing and not quite fighting.

It took a while to collect ourselves, but we eventually talked of the last time we saw each other and how life had been for us over the years. I told them of my journey through the jail system, rehab, then onto sobriety, school, married life, and a professorship. They told me of their blue-collar factory jobs, getting screwed over by temporary agencies, police brutality, house ownership and renting, the once-booming Alberta oil fields, and my one mate who'd done alright, running his own concrete-forming business.

JD's tattoo commemorating his brother's death caught my eye amid our conversation. I recognized a jailhouse tattoo the instant I saw it—no doubt done with ash, water, and a guitar string. It was from only a few months prior, JD had said when I asked him about it, but the ink edges were already bleeding away, the letters already shapeshifting into bugs. I attempted to make out the death date as he invited me to pump iron in the garage like old times. I obliged him and said I'd return soon enough. I don't think he believed me.

As I was leaving, my friends told me they were proud of my success and that I had found a way out. But I was prouder of them because they're still together, and they had the guts and fortitude to live in that place, Brampton. A place I was never strong enough to live in, a place that almost killed me, a place where gladiators and writers are made.

*

The poems in this section are of the people I lost to the streets, or those still out there running drug houses, in addictive addiction, the homeless, in organized crime or in jail. These are my street family and they love(d) me dearly, I am told, for I made it out to become something more than what we were. The places and people contained in this section, however, might scare you, or might even cause you to judge them or the validity of this work. But that is exactly the point. I write for the disabled, the judged, the lower classes, the disenfranchised youth, the blue-collar worker, the gang members, the struggling addict, the street wives, the boy who has to steal to catch a girl's attention, the adoptees who don't always "Indigenous" right, and the criminals mired in our city's drug trade. I write for them in a language they know and understand. I write for them because *I once was them, and parts of me still are*. I have carried them with me, like the story you'll read of Zoltan and his sweater, which has inspired so much of my homelessness advocacy. In this section, I write their poems—poems to humanize my loved ones, and poems so the world can witness their dark beauty and the brutal shadows they cast upon my glimmering shield.

CERBERUS

I went by one of the old trap houses awhile back.
I still know many associates down there,
those who live by favours
and loyalty
and fear.

This last time, as I pulled up,
out came the boys
one by one,
swollen from weights
tatted up
and fresh from provincial.

We could hardly contain ourselves
as I made my way up the driveway
then
all at once
the dogs erupted in chorus
ran and leapt
jaws snapping in front of my face
just as the chains went taught.

I realized then
that the boys might remember me
but these dogs of war
these guardians of Hades
they do not.

When we met, all those years later
you were shuffling around looking for a fix,
your eyes tired and grey,
not the old blazing blue I remember,
not the ferocious woman you once were.

I apologized for life then—
for the way things were
for my alcoholic rage
the yelling
the broken promises and lies.
A thousand times I wished I could have taken it all back.
A thousand times I begged God to let you know I didn't
    mean any of it.

A flicker of the old you flashed across your pupils—
you were still there.
"I forgive you," you said, behind that eternal smile.
You were always such a good Christian girl
so quick to forgive, so quick to love.

"We were lovers in a tumultuous time," you imparted, "so
    long ago now."

It was true, life was hard for us back then.
Addicted and reckless, young and lustful,
but that's no excuse.

"Who's this?"

"My boyfriend . . . he—"

I cut you off before you could finish.
I couldn't stand to hear you lie,
not then, not like that, not on the boulevard where you
waved to every passerby,
searching for something.

But that was two years ago
and I'm here driving down this street
chasing a faded memory of you
hoping life's been better to you
and that you're still alive.

There used to be this old man
who visited the drop-in centre
we all went to for sandwiches
and to do our laundry.

The others would whisper
that this old fella used to drop his daughter
on this corner
decades ago
until one day, just after he dropped her off, she was hit by
    a car and died.

In despair, he lost everything;
his mind;
his heart;
became homeless.

Now,
every day—
if he's still doing it, if he's still alive—
he waits there
searching for her
with her favorite teddy bear in hand
waiting to pick her up.

She became a paramedic—
I knew her in high school
years before this addiction bound me in shackles.
Many times, at Kennedy and Queen,
in the dead of night,
she was the only person
there, in her ambulance
as I scoured the streets for change
and maybe a little money.

She noticed one evening,
me, alone and waiting for a midnight bus that wasn't coming.
"Come clean up at my place," she said, as if stardust was
    caught up in her hair.
I don't know how she drove with me all ripe in the
    passenger seat.
She let me shower when we got to her place
offered the couch
gave me twenty dollars, a pack of smokes
and let me tell her of a man who used to live
inside this old heart.

She turned off the lamp after
and went to bed in the next room.
As quiet sank in, I stole away in the night
ashamed that I had nothing to offer
this girl I once went to school with.
This girl who still cared to remember
this, the paramedic-saint of Peel Memorial;
a hospital they tore down
many years ago.

HOOLIGAN

I owned nothing but the shelter lice on my back,
the damaged poetry within.
And there you were on that calm August day, so beautiful.

When you flashed me a smile,
I loved you instantly
heart dancing with feathers ablaze.

There was something about you,
your doe eyes,
and how your Doc Martens never got dirty, even slumming
    it with me in the gutter.

I wanted to give you the world, but could offer you nothing.
It left me with little choice.

And, so, with these two crafty hands and fast feet
I went out and I thieved for you.
I risked my life and my freedom; I stole kingdoms for you.

"I love them, my king," is what you did say:
"The pauper, the thief,
made me queen for today!"

ERIC

In Peel court holding cells
I saw you.
A long mullet cascading down your shoulders
a glint of mischief still in your eye.

We did pushups together, shaky yet strong
to soothe our anxiety
before our dance with the judge
at our separate hearings.

To my great surprise,
I was released from the box.
You got two years less a day—
that was the last time I saw you.

I googled your name today, ten years later.
An obituary popped up—I never pictured you with kin,
    somehow.
I always saw you like me, a tumbleweed in a Western,
a gunslinger, alone.

As I read the comments from loved ones
I realized: you never could live on the outside.
And it left me asking myself:
I wonder how abolition helps people like you?

CHRISTOPHER

"She left me," you said.
I watched as your world fell in upon itself.
Our faces numb from cocaine; your heart raw and aching.
Your tears out of place in this hardened quarry of white
    rocks and crack stems.

You'd dated her since high school
and we all thought
if any couple was made in heaven
it was you two.

You never gave an explanation of why she went.
You tried to tell me
but your chin just wagged,
with your black, vacant pupils right down to the ocean floor.

Even without words,
I knew her absence caused your Elysian fields to rust.
And you died that night, searching for answers
as Beres Hammond's "Rockaway" played across the
    dope spot.

These streets remember
the time you wrapped your wings
around that wandering soul.
The one with the long face
the injured leg
the empty pockets
and broken heart.
You took the time to listen,
and listening to the judged just isn't in style anymore.
But you did it.
Then you offered your last dollar,
and laughed at the thought of paying you back.
While others around
stepped over our panhandling places on the sidewalk
and turned away
you anointed our feet with oil
washed our heads with kindness
and lived amongst those who needed you most.
I'm no religious expert
but I'm pretty sure I knew a saint
the real kind
who loves without fear
whose millions of selfless acts go unrecorded
but whose star I remember

because it remains
one of the brightest in the firmament
years after you've gone.

Thank you for being kind while others were not.

ZOLTAN

With nowhere to go
I stole your sweater
to stay warm that cold winter night.
It left you with nothing.
Sometime later
I heard you left this world.
Of all the crimes I committed
this one stands as one of the greatest.
Truly, the best of us did not survive.

BRAMPTON

Queen and Kennedy
is the true heart
not Four Corners
everyone knows that.

Suburban dreams of greasy factories
endless warehouses
lawns clipped down in obsession
flowers spilled out and covering scars.

Purple City vision quests still blind the youth
beside the old church that hands out sandwiches
to the dispossessed
every Sunday.

That post-WWII-social-engineering cheese is all served up
on a McKay beef patty.
And, as any real Bramptonian knows:
Bramalea is a foreign country
its barbarous border—the 410 highway.

Saskatoon berries

Part Three

★

LOVE LETTERS FROM REHAB

My pathway off the streets to writing poetry was not normal.

I came before a judge in 2008 who said I could do my dead-time (pretrial custody) at a Christian rehabilitation called Harvest House in Ottawa. I had a severe poly-addiction to crack, alcohol, and oxy then. All of it led to a break-and-enter charge that landed me in hot water in court. The only reason I went to Harvest House is because they were literally the only rehab that would bail me out from provincial custody imme-diately; and this, after I'd relapsed from there a few months earlier. It certainly wasn't because I was religious. They had a trained paralegal who provided this one critical pathway into treatment and I saw my advantage. Every other one that I called couldn't bail me or they had long waiting lists, or they only took people with work insurance, of which I did not have as a street person. The Christianity of the place sat uneasy with me, however. I don't really believe in the Bible but see the wisdom in it—it's really just a library of Hebrew oral stories passed down for thousands of years before they were written down in the Hellenistic period; I value those stories like moral tales or compasses for living, not their divinity. Some of this stuff is completely backwards, I know that, but some of it rings true, even today. But none of that mattered because the truth of it is it really doesn't matter what the person handing you the sandwich believes in when you are at your lowest. You just want to eat.

Life at Harvest House, even with tasty sandwiches, wasn't easy.

From sun-up to sundown I did chores and school—cleaning the washrooms, cooking and running the kitchen, waxing the floors, and going to GED classes. I also had to cold call strangers and sell calendars to pay for my room and board; $20 a pop. I sold around five a night, the other addicts around three. Panhandling for years gave me quite the advantage. Harvest House is a private institution so they make poorer clients pay for their own stay and bail, something quite different than provincial rehabs paid for by the government or work insurance. The compound was a mix of broke rounders and jailbirds like myself, and others who had their family's supplement part of their stay out of pocket. They always sold less than us street folk. Cold-calling, even if you had money, was a necessary part of the social skills building part of the program. It helped with stress management and was so when you hit freedom and came up against massive stress, you'd be able to handle life on life's terms and wouldn't use or react. I mean, what's more stressful than a recovering addict ringing someone up out of the blue, interrupting their dinner, and begging them for money? Oh, the earfuls we'd get, but at the same time we gained negotiation and mediation skills—some of the guys were so good after a while that they could calm down an irate person and then turn them into a monthly doner. My buddy Burnt McBurnt was one such man—one of the only guys to outsell me on cold calls.

Another part of the program was professional development (PD) class. Every Monday and Wednesday for two hours, us clients sat in a giant circle. The counsellors used to get us to write down various things that made us ashamed or hurt or resentful, so when we were called to stand in PD, we could share and grow in the circle with the others. Resentments, they told us, drove addiction and disconnection, and in PD we were expected to broadcast our traumas, our scars, to the other addicts, while also admitting we were liars, thieves, and cheats, and to confront the naked truth of who we actually were as criminals (this was mainly for the jail guys). None of this coddling that actually kills people who must face their truth or die. I've seen those counsellors—themselves former heavies so you can't bullshit them—break straight-up murderers in this way, but also build them back up into kind, loving, and generous people. PD was like chrysalid class. I'd just sit there in awe watching caterpillars turn into butterflies before my very eyes. And the narrative therapy model we partook in made sense of the chaos of trauma and addiction. The human brain is story-driven and to chronologically order pain in a coherent and linear narrative helps addicts sort through and make sense of the infinite disruptions and discombobulations of active addictions. Imagine trying to drive down the highway in a straight line with a blindfold on—all that steering out of your lane, all that incoherent trauma coming from every direction, all that collision—that's active addiction. You take off the blindfold with narrative story so you're not in a constant car crash and you can actually see where you're going as well as where you've been.

Ordering our traumas and survival behavior was what PD was all about; we wrote down our resentments on these 3-by-6 cue cards and matched them with a Bible verse describing something similar. I did my cards faithfully while serving my deadtime, and each time I thought I'd shared the worst parts of my addictions, I realized that the others in the circle had their own gruesome stories of deprivation and abandonment. Much of it far worse than mine. Sharing so deeply was freeing and created fellowship for the participating addicts, who saw their journeys in my own, as I did in theirs. It was in this gruelling and very public way, with those cards, that we came to love one another and repair some of the damage that drove our addictions.

So here I am this criminal-addict chiselling my worst memories into these cue cards and stuttering in therapy—honestly the hardest thing I've ever done—all while trying to improve my reading in GED classes, and staying up late every night with my nose in a set of encyclopedias I'd borrowed from the rec room. I was functionally illiterate and was trying anything to improve. As time passed, I noticed I was becoming quite articulate. Some of the fragmented things I'd say in PD would suck the air out of the room, or make others gasp out loud or cry. They said I had a way with words.

Things continued like this for a good seven months until I couldn't sleep one night because my left wrist throbbed. I went to the walk-in clinic with my escort and the doctor informed me that I had a broken wrist that needed reconstruction surgery. It was an old scaphoid break—from four years earlier when I'd fallen off a three-and-a-half-story building, and when I'd gotten into a fist fight with a bunch of undercovers and uniformed policeman two years after that. The doctor also told me it wasn't very smart to do 200 push-ups a day—something I'd done in jail and rehab, despite the pain, to protect myself. A few weeks after my consultation, I had the operation.

I was released with a hydro-morphine prescription and a cast on my left wrist. I didn't tell the rehab I had the meds, and that night I relapsed alone in my dorm bed. When morning hit, I walked to the office and told on myself, handed in my meds, and waited to get kicked out.

Hey, I reasoned, *I got in seven months; I got some of my resentments out on these cards, and I am healthy. I don't mind being sent back to the Can.*

That's what I deserve.

Strangely, however, nothing happened. I was later told that my drug use that night technically wasn't a relapse because I actually needed the pain medication for once. And right after that, my grandma Jackie died, and I graduated and was placed in reintegration housing where I was to start finding my way in the world under supervision from escorts, chaperones, and work placement. They gave me a computer to use and I started a Facebook profile. One of the first messages I got was from a girl named Lucie I knew from way back in junior high school. I thought her condolence was just about the kindest thing anyone could've done for me then—you all will read the poem it inspired in a few pages. It didn't hurt that she was hot and had deep red hair—I've always had a thing for redheads.

I had pretty much nothing when she started speaking with me. I owned maybe a half a dresser of clothes from the donation bin, thousands of personal hygiene products (it is a long story but the short version is that they were a reaction to trauma), my blue jail shoes I kept to remind me where I came from, my jail underwear, and a brown leather jacket I bought with the weekly allowance I'd saved during my time in rehab. I truly had jack, but she didn't seem to mind. As we got to know one another, it was Hotmail Messenger or Skype every night, or we'd talk on the phone long distance for hours. Our courtship was like that—we took our time, like they used to do a long time ago, in simpler times.

I started small, firing off poetic trifles on the spot. They just flowed out of me, live, and from the excited feeling that bubbled every time I talked with her; a girl I knew was way out of my league. And she seemed to like what I wrote, commenting with a heart emoji or a poem by e e cummings or a picture of herself smiling or a video of her apartment in Toronto. It was so nice to hear her encouragement and thanks—she made me believe I could write. And it made me feel like I—this mega-loser for life—had something of value, my words, if that makes any sense. There were times she messaged back and said I was a natural poet, or that I was her little Shakespeare, or she'd send me letters drenched in perfume that I'd wait for from the mailman.

She just appreciated me and it gave me back some of my dignity and pride. Poems, in this context, nourished me, freed me, and out of them grew love.

So that's how it was and that's what I did—I wrote an avalanche of poems from minimum security rehab/jail while serving my one year. I typed them on Messenger with my one free hand, the other in a cast—I bled for each and every word I sent her. My primary goal—let's face it—was to get in Lucie's pants (I was just a jailbird then, I can admit that) but that changed over time into a genuine and lasting affection for her heart and mind, ideas and words.

I know it is anticlimactic, but that's the simple story of how I came to write poetry. One minute I'm trying to get bail, the next I'm writing on these cue cards in rehab, and the next I'm sending poems to this kind girl from back in the day.

*

Fast forward a decade, I hadn't thought of those poems for years, and we culled from my own collection only what would strengthen my life story for *From the Ashes*. It is not an easy feat to sparsely pick poems and narrow down forty years of life into a coherent meta-narrative that was both entertaining and wasn't 1200 pages. We must've picked well as many readers commented specifically on the strength of the poetry—how it was their favorite part of the book—how they wanted a collection of Thistle poems alone.

Seeing all this positive reaction, my wife Lucie knew what to do. As if by magic one day, she opened an old Word file on her desktop. It was the cache of poems I'd sent her way back in 2009 when I was still trying to win her heart—I thought she'd erased them years ago as I'd done.

She believed they were publishable—I read them and thought she might have bonked her head, but sent them off to my agent Sam anyway. Turns out Lucie was right. They were pretty good. Sam had no trouble punting my stardust poetry. Proof is that they are here before you, my reader, this archive between lovers, this, the lightest and hottest of our forge's light.

In the temple of the human heart
she laid supplications of kindness.

"I'm sorry to hear your grandmother died," her message
    to me read,
"Is there anything I can do?"

Then.
It was then
I fell
eternally
in love.

Light in Latin
is *Lux*.
She is the light
and
I
the darkness.
When she came into my world
dawn and dusk and daylight lived.
Now we, supernova lovers,
are
forever locked
in the revolution
of
day and night.

Always remember the magnitude of our love,
it has the power to transcend all we see; all that we are
it is our little contribution to the greater good of it all
our love will one day sprout life
of this much I am sure.

WITHOUT WORDS

All I love is in you,
captured in your tones,
your mannerisms.
There's a kindness, an understanding
you need but utter one word
and I know the intention of your heart,
my spirit rendered speechless.

SUPERNOVA

We are but stars
a flicker
in time
burning brightly
hoping someone somewhere will admire
our glitter against the black backdrop of life.
We all shine in this way
distant
yet we shine
in the cold vacuum of space.

A feeling tumbled
off my lips:
"I love you," I said, and from somewhere deep
sweet molasses poured down across our bed.
Then love squeezed
from our lips, wrapped up in sheets
locked and overwhelmed
engulfed in orgasm,
and from behind your teeth a groan,
a queen in her throne.

Soothed in some mystery of slumber
I ingest the substance.
My head is heavy
plumes of fragrant opium dance across my nostrils
expand inside my chest
dulled and at peace.
I've fallen so awake, here, in your arms.
Far far away
from the biting cold
of reality.

VOLCANO

There is a deep eruption welling up
with immense pressure
it threatens to rip up earth
force its way into being.
You've awakened some immeasurable force within
something foreign; a lost refugee; a heart I forgot I had.
A cast of light lifts off the nape of your neck
shining a strange and wonderous feeling—
this land that time forgot.
There I plead
stuttering words of Eros
a geography I barely understand.

HUNGRY

The glossy sheen upon your lips
refracts the light   in such a way   as to mimic
            the glistening
                of moon beams   off a calm ocean at midnight.

Can I indulge in their mystic?

Just one taste,
        to savour their plumpness.

Oh me
    how I want to devour them.

BETWEEN LOVERS

It was only a whisper
floating and fleeting
and from off our tongues
a phoenix rose forth
that wrought death and destruction.
Fire engulfed the city
scorched the sky
salted the ground
but, here, it all grew
a moment in time,
a moment of lust shared between lovers.

A murmur on the horizon—
I am in the trenches
fighting my private war.
My body longs to hear your affection
my mind yearns to touch yours.
If I concentrate enough
the artillery and guns fade away
and I can feel you beside me
a thousand miles away.

My lovely hyacinth
daughter of Zeus and Leda
you command empires
like Xerxes once did.

Last I saw you
ten thousand ships launched to Troy
and I watched, lovesick
yearning that I might win your hand.

But that was a long time ago
and here at last I find you
across oceans of time and the Aegean
my one and last chance to truly live immortal.

SUNKEN TREASURE

The grandeur of life is apparent in all the little details.
You miss those sailing after extravagant delusions—
the small way you smile
the tiny sound of your laugh
the way your eyes shine like Crab Nebulas when you're
interested in something.
Those are my minute treasures, each one a gold coin, each
    one a carved emerald
and I search lost shipwrecks for them—for you
and I claim them as such.

BERRY PICKING

Hope, my love,
it burns brightest of all.
So vibrant—
scattering the wreckage of my past
you illuminate the forest.
Now I can pluck those kisses and carry them
to sustain me for the journey ahead.
One by one
I shall savour them
like wild berries
in harvest.

SEA GLASS

Fractured and cloudy,
the light shone through
when she held it
up
to the sun.

The violence of the ocean
had smoothed
the sharp edges of his youth.

She plucked him one day
there,
on a random stretch of beach.
A worn piece of sea glass
hidden
amongst the drift pile.

With kindness and care
she laid siege to these walls
of obsidian and granite
laid brick by massive brick by the Byzantines.

And the most surprising thing
is she did this all as if by fate,
without even trying.

It was just a simple smile, but it crashed upon me like
     Mehmet II and the hulking cannon fire of the Ottomans,
a solid brass missile from this unassuming girl,
and it blew away my unconquerable citadel,
my deserted Constantinople.

STAR CATCHER

She is my astrolabe
she knows every star;
she knows places close to us
she knows places far.

She took us to Prague once
then Starbucks down the road
and we always have mega fun
on the adventures we know!

She always charts the vast heavens
on the way there and the way back,
and she tracks out their orbits
for the thousands of stars that we catch.

L is for love, lush and lovely, laughing and listening, since the moment we met.

O is for optimism, forever offering ourselves, overjoyed and open-hearted.

V is for vow, a vocalization we made to Creator and one another, vigorous and vibrant.

E is for everlasting—enduring through eternity, our endearment effortless and enamoured, endlessly enchanting each other.

I, her servant and lover,
pray daily at her temple with pious reverence
and devotion in her sacred chamber.
I approach her altar with supplications
and libation and from her breast
out pours boundless milk and honey
to sustain mine being.
I burn incense
and rub myrrh and oil into the feet
of my Goddess,
the mother of Horus
daughter of Nut and Geb.
She commands life and bounty
upon the banks of the Nile
and in the halls of our home.
Oh, how lucky I am to have married Isis
and to enjoy her fortunes and favours.

*This a reworking of an ancient Egyptian love poem from the
New Kingdom (1550-1069 BCE)*

Sage

Part Four

*

FORGOTTEN TOBACCO

My first job when I got sober and was released from rehab was as a potato smasher and dishwasher at Poutini's on Queen West in Toronto. Potato smashers feed potatoes through a press to make french fries. I got the job after Lucie and I bumped into her friends Nick, Fred, and Katie, the owners of Poutini's. They said they needed a guy to smash potatoes and wash dishes, that it was a hard and unglamorous job, and that they couldn't pay that much because of the nature of the work. I understood, and as an ex-convict I was lucky to find employment.

By the time our conversation was over, I felt I had the job. A while later they called and I had an interview, and the next day I was smashing potatoes into fries for Toronto's best poutinery.

When I first started, the fifty-pound boxes of potatoes were heavy and the work of washing and pruning the potatoes, then pressing them through the fry press, was onerous. It was wet and made my hands raw and I stunk like a giant rotten potato every night when I got home.

A strange thing occurred halfway through the first week. I noticed that if I maximized the way I lifted the boxes of potatoes, I could increase my speed, lessen my workload, and save my back a lot of pain. The same thing applied when I washed the potatoes—I learned the kinds of potatoes and soils I was working with, and could soon de-eye potatoes in seconds flat.

Two weeks in and I developed a method where I could hold four potatoes in one hand and feed them through the smasher while I operated the press with my other hand. Thump, thump, thump, thump was the sound it made. I called this potato smashing method 'The Howitzer' after the "BOOM" of the famous World War II artillery gun; one round was a quarter bucket of freshly cut fries ready for the fryer.

By the end of my first month, I'd transformed into a fiddler crab—these crabs have one huge arm and one small one. The constant pressing of the machine had caused my right arm to become huge and veiny while my left arm remained normal-sized feeding the smasher. One night I smashed nineteen bins of potatoes, a record that remained at Poutini's until they closed shop.

By the time I left Poutini's, I loved that job and the people there and greatly appreciated the chance they gave me right out of rehab. But I took away something much more important. I learned that you've got to do your best in whatever you do, even if it's smashing potatoes and washing dishes, and even if your job leaves you stinking like a giant rotten potato and you look like a lopsided sea crustacean after a while, because every chance you get in life deserves respect, and so do the people who took chances on you like Poutini's and Lucie did with me. You do that by showing up and trying your hardest each and every day—cutting fries taught me that.

★

The paragraphs above capture the humble beginnings of my sobriety in 2009. The piece was written in 2013 and represents a fulcrum in this book as we move from nostalgic pieces that romanticize street life to fuller prose and poems that detail my rise and recovery, my reintegration back into society after almost eleven years cycling in and out of homelessness. They start by showing you the fears and triumphs of a baby-legged man who started, literally, from the bottom up, cleaning toilets in rehab—a dangerous job that exposed me to hepatitis daily (many guys in rehab have Hep C or Hep A).

Next, I move in with Lucie and cut french fries, build kitchens in people's homes, dance over top of my Achilles tendon injury, and start university. Indeed, the insecurities and doubts of a newly emerged criminal-addict integrating back into regular sober life appear here—taking my girl to a nice meal, mundane traffic stops, lingering PTSD, learning empathy, and reckoning with past ghosts—friends and associates—who are still stuck down in Hades. This section, then, leads naturally into the deep cultural ambivalence I fight against as an adoptee raised outside of his maternal Métis-Cree culture, but who came back to it in his mid-thirties in an attempt to reconnect with his mother and stay sober. I show you through poems how I struggled with traditional ceremony, rewriting myopic historical narratives, going back home to Saskatchewan, and the fear of disappearing like my father did. Life was not a piece of cake while cleaning up. There was so much going on then, and these poems, first recorded on my cue cards, often have a disjointed feeling or relationship to one another. This was a conscious choice in organization and was done to highlight how picking up the pieces is a confusing and disorganized myriad task, especially if one's disabled, traumatized, and not sure of oneself. Being ordered this way, in glancing staccato prose, is supposed to mimic the unsure strikes of when I first learned to wield Hephaestus's hammer in written word.

A NICE MEAL

In the Byward Market
there's a fancy seafood restaurant.
I'd sit outside and panhandle
catching patrons one by one.

I vowed if I ever cleaned up,
found a place in the world,
I'd come right back here
and buy the biggest lobster in the tank.

Some years ago, but after I decided to live again,
Lucie and I drove back there.
It didn't look as menacing as before, somehow
the concrete transformed back into just sidewalk.

My lobster tasted wonderful that night,
Lucie's, the same.
And even now I can't put my finger on it, of how deeply
        this all affected me
this memory drenched in butter, this nice meal with my girl.

When I look down at my tired and sore hands in the midst of my labours, covered in stone chips and sawdust, sweat and blood, I don't see the thick callouses that leather my palms like old well-worn catcher's mitts. Nor do I see the many hundreds of scars—big and small—from a thousand stubborn jobs and mistakes. And I don't see the arthritic joints that restrict me from working as hard as I did when I was twenty. No. When I look down at my hands through dust and debris, I see my golden wedding ring and the promise of love that it carries, I see the life that it represents, and I see the dreams that live upon it. I see you, my lovely Lucie. Then, all at once, my weathered hands become invigorated, instantly as young and light and strong as they once were. When I look down in my toils, I see that ring and I remember why I work so hard.

PTSD

I smell the flowers
in my backyard
but still think
behind each petal
each blade of grass
each impossibly skinny tree trunk
lay gunmen
and goblins
and police with red lasers pointed
right at my chest.

Dishonoured,
I got down on my knees,
unsheathed the blade,
thrust it into my torso,
turned it,
then pulled the hilt up and towards my chin
and completed the gruesome task.

To my surprise
it was not blood and pain and death that gushed forth,
but beautiful words and poems and stories
spraying life onto the page.

Earlier this week I was pulled over for running a stop sign. After I gave the officer my name and licence, he ran a full background check on me in his squad car, then sent my profile off to division dispatch for further inspection. He kept glaring at me; he didn't look pleased.

I was there maybe thirty-five minutes. Thirty minutes longer than a normal stop.

When he approached the car, he had his hand over his sidearm. He looked vigilant and on guard. He handed back my licence and said, "Well, you haven't been in trouble for quite some time, Mr. Thistle. That's good. What you been up to?" His eyes sussed me out.

"Oh, I got clean," I said through the side of my mouth.

"Turned in my oranges. I'm in university currently, getting my PhD. I'm like you now, I guess—trying to do good, help society for a change."

A smile lit up his face.

"Really?" He looked relaxed but confused, and glad for me all the same.

"Yeah. I was never meant to be that person you see in that file."

He recomposed himself. "Keep up the good work, son," he said then handed me my tickets and slapped my side mirror, as if saying we were all done.

"But it still doesn't absolve you from these two tickets here.

One for running the stop sign, the other for not having your insurance on your person. Contest them. Sometimes the prosecutors reduce or drop them, and sometimes the cops don't even show up."

With that he turned and walked away.

I appear in traffic court soon. I'm not sure what will happen, but I'm hopeful.

If you listen
hard enough
you can see
their tears
in the rainfall
and feel their cries
in the silence.

But you must listen.

I learned empathy during my stay at Harvest House. They had me feed Ledbury hood boxes of old produce thrown away by neighbouring grocery stores. Ledbury sits in a food desert and has no access to healthy fruits and vegetables. It was part of my program to feed those in places I used to steal from. One day this poem came to me after I gave an old lady an apple. I don't know, it was the way she looked at me, I ran from her and wept under a tree. I just couldn't stop. I realized then, in my core, the damage I'd done to good people all along. I believe that feeling that day, that spirit of empathy, that old lady, was an angel; and I feel this because it changed my heart and the feeling of wanting to help has never left me and I can still see her face.

WHAT MATTERS

Quality of mind
can only achieve so much
it is only quality of heart
that truly achieves greatness.

LITTLE BOY BROOM

There's this blonde kid
just two or three years old
across the street from us.

We watch every now and again as he tussles on his grass
plays with his aunties and mum
or when he's out there working—he treats it like a full-time gig.

We noticed him one day with his granddad
dirty as hell
chucking leaves on the back of the pick-up truck
little dude tried so hard
but his arms couldn't reach.

Another time the tiny lad was hauling wood
a branch five times his torso—
when he hoisted it to the refuse pile, he fell over—
bloodied up his knees, but he kept on smiling
all to impress his granny.

And today he sits there
tuckered out
atop the stairs
broom in one hand, the other clad in a gardener's glove
    many sizes too big.

This a job he does, like all the others,
a chance to help his family,
and especially his dear mother.

FOOTLOOSE

The foot turns in now
doesn't carry the weight it used to.
My limp slants my body, tilts shoulders,
but tells a story.

And when the clouds hang low like today
and are swollen with tears,
my metal ankle they put in
swells and bites and makes it difficult to walk.

Then. It is then we must turn up the stereo
—as loud as it goes
and dance in the living room until our bones cry
—and in that we gnash against the years, and all our fears.

I got a call in 2018 from Harvest House, the place that got me sober in 2009.

The caller's voice was familiar. It was Burnt McBurnt, a slick-mouthed hustler I was in treatment with years ago. He'd fallen on rough times again, relapsed, and was back in rehab. He was now sober, he told me, and running marathons again, and that was good. And he was also cold calling folks to pay for his stay at rehab, like I used to, which meant he was in the earliest stages of recovery—the most special and hardest part.

"It's difficult to give it another shot," I said. "I'm proud you found the courage again."

"Thanks buds," he said, likely mulling over his last attempt at rehab back when he was my roomy, "but why haven't you donated in all the years you've been away? You too good for us now?"

I had no answer. I sat there frozen.

How could I forget? I thought. *I'm so bloody self-absorbed.*

It troubled me.

McBurnt kept pressing. "If you don't tell me soon," he said, "I'll sic Randal on you for the cash. Pony up the dough, you ungrateful degenerate." I missed being talked to rough like a criminal; I missed my people. I still had no answer.

Randal is my old AA sponsor, the guy who took me to see my grandmother when she was dying in 2009. "Holy cheapskate, Batman," he said as he got on McBurnt's phone; it was a relief to hear Randal's voice after almost a decade away. But I knew I was in shit.

I tried sidestepping the Jehovah's Witness-like pressure by thanking him for stowing me away in the Ottawa moving truck and whisking me to Toronto to see my grandma two weeks before she died. Randal was my chaperone that crucial night, and I would not have been allowed to go if it wasn't for him—I was not allowed to leave city limits on such harsh bail conditions. And I was lucky he agreed, too. That trip was the last time I'd see my grandmother alive. Escorting me to Toronto was something Randal didn't have to do. He'd done it because he was a good guy and he knew how much saying goodbye in the right way meant to me and my sobriety.

That last visit to see Grandma in the oncology ward, as it turns out, was one of the most important moments of my life. For it was then that I promised my grandmother Jackie that I'd get my education and clean up my act, it was then that I promised to go to university. That promise has guided me in all of my current success, through all the peaks and valleys over the past thirteen years, and right into a professorship at one of the country's leading universities.

When I thanked Randal again for that clandestine night to visit Grandma, he played it cool, "No sweat—that's just what brothers do," he said, and changed the topic back to how I was so cheap. We then made fun of guys we got sober with years ago; how they stank, ate everything in sight, and were dirtballs who lacked basic human hygiene. But through our non-emotive guy-talk and jest, I knew he understood how much that trip meant to me and how thankful I was.

Before he hung up, I felt compelled to donate what I could as a token of appreciation for the second chance Harvest House and Randal gave me.

He then got the guys at the rehab centre to shout a collective "thank you" for my donation into the phone. It was something I remembered doing back in the day, and it felt nice to be on the other side, nice to give back. Those small twenty-dollar donations really do save lives.

When I think of all the dudes I got sober with—many now dead, in jail, or still out there—I realize that I owe Randal the biggest thanks for what he did that night in February 2009. It was my one chance to say goodbye to my grandmother, my one chance to repair our relationship. Though I must say, his choice of hockey team sucks. I mean, how can any self-respecting Ontarian like the Ottawa Senators over the Toronto Maple Leafs? How, I ask? No one's perfect, I guess.

DUST

Sitting
drinking my coffee
I realize
in 200 years
no one will know
or care
if any of us lived
which means
we only have today
to dance up clouds of dust.

FORGOTTEN TOBACCO

I don't remember too much about Dad
he left when I was three
but I remember cigarettes—he smoked.
Dad never had much money though,
addictions and whatnot, needles,
but I remember he'd go around
picking up castaway butts off the street
then come home and roll them up.

—brown and yellow fingers —

and the stale smell
of old half-smoked cigarettes would fill our empty apartment,
rotten and damp.

I still love the smell of discarded tobacco
all tangled up in a homeless man's beard,

sacred.

FATHER

Another day passes
and I search for you
scouring old newspapers
microfiche
and John Doe death rolls
and when I pass homeless men
on the boulevard
around your age
I ask if them if they are you
if they, somehow, are Sonny Thistle—my dad.

It's illogical
but still
I search for you
just as any son would
a stalwart champion for his disappeared father.

ONCOLOGY WARD

I sit on your deathbed, Grandmother.
You're gaunt
with eyes sunken in
hollow cheeks
orbital and mandible bones sticking out
as you chew your food.

You don't look so well now,
at the end of winter's season.
That eternal sun that lit up your youth
has set behind old age.

Your hospital gown hangs
like wind-torn sea sails
strewn across storm-broken masts.

But there's defiance left in you,
a glowing ember
a spark
a flicker
a flame.

"Have courage, dear grandson," you said, your eyes
    meeting mine,
"we'll beat this cancer yet."

Many years after it took you,
a part of me still thinks you can beat it.
A part of me knows that you did.

GRANDMA

I found an old photograph of you today
faded and yellow
from the '80s or earlier.
You're just like I remember:
waxed-paper grandma-skin, polyester slacks, and wondrous
    grey-black permed afro.
Sometimes I wonder if you guide me to these lost relics,
these photographs,
these forgotten remnants of you,
just to assure me that you're still with me,
that you're still around.

She knits in silence
recalling her child
when first they rode down the street
wind and wonder whizzing through their hair
those training wheels off.

She stares
out the window
to that spot by the lake
just off the rickety dock
in early summer
where they first learned to swim.

She waits
in her rocking chair, the years given way to tears,
holding her holy relic
hoping for a child's return.
And wishing, when it happened, God was with you and that
    you weren't alone.

In memory of my grandma who waited.
In memory of my father who never came home.

Inside was great.
Sometimes they had these dentists that'd come
into the jail
and fix the inmates' teeth.

They came in monthly to assess who needed what repair;
I'd put requests in with programs,
show them my one broken and black snaggletooth— the
    very front right bucktooth—
and get my appointment.

Sometimes I'd celebrate that I was caught
on a theft under charge—a cup of coffee bid—
because it meant, apart from the food and bug juice
    (psychotropic medication) and seeing my friends,
I could smile again with some dignity.

It kind of makes me sad to think about now,
how pitiful that all was,
but I won't lie:
apart from the birth of my baby and my marriage and
    writing poems and stories

Lesson learned.

Here is the hard-won poem that emerged, and the vision I had out there on the Great Plains in 2018.

Placed upon the land
in my lodge
we sweated.
The plump Saskatoon berries
teased my hunger
for four long nights
dangling and dancing in the bush.
No water; no food.
I sucked the earth for moisture.
Wrapped in ancestral kokum love
I transformed into a toad.
When they came for me
I collapsed; me heart gave out.
A relative born anew.

LATERAL TITHING

I watch your plate
it looks good
what you got there.
Here
in the colonial jungle.

I watch your plate.
Envy drives
guiding my eyes to you and your plate.
Here, inside my wretched kingdom.

I watch your plate.
I cannot believe a peasant is eating while I—the monarch of
    this realm—am not.
I reach over
grab the juiciest morsel from in front of you
and eat it in your face
then I burp.

What the fuck are you going to do?
Argue with my fist or gun, or worse, my entitlement?

You watch my plate
you cannot believe
I just took what I wanted
took everything from you
and it happened
just like that.

We together watch their plates now,
the plates of the Others.
For you learned to steal power from me,
learned to steal it from them,
as I once did
when *they* took everything from my plate
and forced me to turn on those close to me.

I guess, looking back, I can see
that we really did learn well from the Church.
Those lessons of shame, of scarcity,
of destroying each other for little gain, to get
    ahead a bit.
It was they who taught us that if we take from
    Peter's plate
we might get some.
But ultimately, we enrich their coffers
because it makes us weak and disunited

and none of us has anything to eat but them,
far off and safe in the next room while we fight
    over crumbs.

Don't we realize we're doing exactly as they want us to?

Note: I do not actually own a gun.

I take your statues, your heroes,
of hate
and power
and generations of stolen land
and forced labour
and we throw it into our
oceans of love
and knowledge
and monuments fall like stacks of dominoes.
Finally, after whole forests of stone and bronze have felled,
and rains quench the Earth,
our narrative is told.
This—after worlds
and injustices
and lifetimes apart.

THE BISON STAMPEDE

There are times in my sleep,
or awake at my desk,
that I feel a stampede
of bison running deep in my chest.
I hear the buzz of the flies that live on their backs.
I feel the ground tremble, quake, and crack.
I see the dust cloud rise at the kick of their hooves.
And I hear grunts and groans and watch the herd move.
These feelings run through me, carry me, invigorate me,
    and remind me:
The great herds have not disappeared,
they merely live in the hearts of Indigenous Plains people,
and they will soon run again.

I once found an eagle feather
in the parking lot of a McDonald's.
It was a little greasy
and smelled like hash browns
but I loved it.

The molted plumage was a chance to express myself
a chance to know my mother's Métis-Cree people
who'd been lost to me
way back in my troubled childhood.

I took it all over—to ceremonies
to smudge and say a prayer over
until one day
an Elder pulled me aside:
"I hate to break it to you, son. But that's not an eagle
     feather.
That's from a seagull."

This is why I never judge someone who is trying to
     reconnect. We are all just trying to grab anything to find
     ourselves, even greasy feathers at Rotten Ronnies.

Reconnection is hard for the disconnected
those raised outside of their Indigenous cultural matrices.
The journey back to ourselves
involves making sense of our scars,
knowing when our tongues have been cut off in some foreign
    colonial witchcraft.

In the years I wandered back to myself,
I gazed upon my roadmap of traumas
and finally saw how it was *they* who took from us our
    beautiful Michif
our dances in the face of the NWMP
and it is their lapdogs who try to shame us for
emerging from empire
emerging from Hades
and emerging from self-hate.

When I returned
home after almost 35 years
an Elder was there.
She caught me as the wind catches milk thistle seed
blowing in the wind.
She does this for many of our wanderers.
The very first thing she made me do is dig
through the earth of my homeland on hand and knee,

to submerge my hands
in the very place my ancestors fought to defend—to ground
    me, at last
and plant myself so I'll never wander again.

As I toiled, she told me of our people
Lii Michif— *Otipemisiwak*, as our Cree relatives would say.
Those brave souls who took up arms against Canadian
    imperialism
at Batoche, Fish Creek, Duck Lake, and the Battlefords.
She said that our clan—the Morrissette-Arcand clan—was
    one of the most militant, the most defiant
and because of it were always the best storytellers and fiddle
    players.
"It's why you and I tell stories," she said, "and why you've
    fought your whole life.
I believe it was to make you tough so when we rise again,
    soon, you'll be strong enough this time around."

This time around, I thought, the brownish red prairie earth
    moving between my fingers. I didn't know what it meant,
    but I knew I'd die fighting for this feeling back to myself
    and my people, a belonging stolen from me as a young boy.

I used to have to take my auntie shopping at the second-hand store quite frequently.

I used to have to fix her porch whenever I came back to Saskatchewan on research.

I used to have to clean her kitchen when the Elders and knowledge keepers had met.

I used to have to fix her roof in early June before the rains.

I used to have to make her a medicine hut, but the one I made wasn't very good.

And I used to have to wash her dishes and split her wood— she's old now and cannot toil like a young lady.

That's the cost of being a Michif person with reciprocal responsibilities to living community members that own you back. This is what makes me Michif. That, and my ancestral biology and political struggle against imperialism from 1816 to 2021.

In return for all the above tasks, I got an onion teaching a few summers ago that I have asked permission to share.

"Yes, us old Michifs," my auntie Maria Campbell began, "we love our onions," she said in a sage way.

"You see, an onion isn't just a vegetable, it has lessons if you just look and listen. You can learn a lot about yourself from an onion. It has layers, you peel one layer back and there's another layer underneath, just like our minds and our stories and our history; if we peel back enough layers of our life, of our subconscious, and of our genealogy, we get back to ourselves, to our core, to our people. That's the centre of the onion and it is the sweetest most vital part of the onion, mmm . . . mmm . . . But you'll do a lot of crying before you get to the centre, that's for sure. And the onion has medicine in it too; it keeps bugs off of the other vegetables which reminds us to protect our kin and to stay close to one another, to help in a good way, it reminds us of our *wahkootawin*. But best of all: Onions taste great and fit into any meal just like us Michif, we can adapt to every situation and make it good. Mmm . . ."

With that, she peeled the outer skin off the onion and took a huge bite of it. I stood there in awe as I watched this lady of seventy-five eat a giant white onion like she was consuming an apple, like I had only ever seen Bruce Lee in his prime eat!

My God, I thought, *we Michif—she—Maria—must be as tough as nails to eat a raw onion like that.*

She just smiled at me, as if she knew I was admiring her onion eating grit and the toughness of our people—the Free People, my people, the People That Own Themselves.

If I go missing, please don't wait to report it to police.
I didn't "run away"
or "make a choice to start a new life"
and neither am I "adventuring"
or "taking a family break"
or "trying to get sober off somewhere"
or "battling my addictions alone"
or off wandering "trying to find myself."

No.

Please don't leap to conclusions if I evaporate into thin air.
Please just report it.
And please hound the police to do their fucking job.
They expunge dental and other identifying evidence after
    ten years.
Don't ask how I know this.

At the foot of the rolling Cape Breton Highlands
we kids would crush rusty red rocks into dust,
mix the deep ocher pigments in our own spit,
then spread the thickness across our faces.

In an instant we became the fiercest warriors that our young
    imaginations could conjure—
a tribe of Conan the Barbarians.

When I look back now,
I think in that moment we *were* invincible.
Scratch that—
I know we were.

Wild prairie roses

Part Five

*

SOMEONE'S ANCESTOR

"You smile more now," my wife Lucie texted me this morning around six-thirty a.m., while I was upstairs working on this very publication. Along with it she sent this meme of a baby giggling with the average daily smiles for humans—babies around 200 times; women, sixty-two; men, eight. I ran downstairs holding my phone. "Do I smile eight times a day?" I said to Lucie. There was a hopeful tone to the way I asked, hovering and out of breath. Perhaps too loudly, though.

I've always imagined myself to be a happy man since 2009, or at least I thought I was, until Lucie said, sadly: "No. There was a while there that you rarely smiled." My face hung like a cold ham sandwich. It hurt to hear.

"But," she giggled, "since Rose was born, you smile more and more." Lucie tilted her head and smiled, the good woman she is, her arms open for a comforting hug.

Rose must've sensed we were talking about her. Only a few feet away on the living room floor, she cooed and reached up toward us from the baby bouncer. Her plump newborn cheeks squeezed up into grape-juice joy; her little arms rotating like helicopter blades. Her laugh was a cross between a sigh and an exaltation broadcast by tiny lungs. Never have I heard a sweeter sound than a newborn learning to laugh.

"See," Lucie commented, "you're doing it right now."

Rose's giggles and the morning sun flooded the room with

love, a warm baptism that anointed the very foundation of our home, and had me grinning like a kid learning to swim at the cottage.

★

Nine-thirty a.m. came in like a brick through my office window—I'd planned to have 2,000 words done by now, but had nothing. I imagined glass shards all over my chair and bookshelf and leaned back so they cut me up good and proper. My coffee cup sat empty beside me; a few grounds left on the bottom, just as vacant as my page—a blizzard inside a blizzard—a few sparse words set against the wall of white.

Writing deadlines always have that effect.

I cannot write. I cannot cannot . . . I . . . I . . . write . . . blarg . . .

I typed these words over and over until black horizontal script polluted the screen like diesel on snowbanks. Halfway down the page, I remembered what Lucie said only hours earlier.

There was a long while there that you didn't smile at all . . .

A pang gripped my chest. I slumped over my desktop and cursed God for tasking me with such an impossible task—follow up *From the Ashes* with something better.

I sat frozen, turned to stone.

Just then, I heard Rose and Lucie running through the cue cards in the next room, the black and white contrast ones that newborns use to train and coordinate their ocular movements; baby's vocal cords also get a good workout.

"And this one is the penguin," Lucie said, her daytime shows droning on in the background. "Rose—look here, see, baby girl—PENGUIN." The penguin card with the waves on the back, I discovered a few days before, was Rose's favorite card by a long shot. She was enjoying it even more with Mommy turning the cards.

Rose paused a second and then gasped and giggled— louder than earlier. She went on for about ten seconds and I picked up my phone and opened the selfie feature, hoping to capture my smile. There it was again, an old and tired smile, as if Jesus himself had resurrected Lazarus's now two thousand-year-old smile and plastered it across my ugly mug. I looked ridiculous. I imagined Jay-Z fighting back happiness as I counted what was my second impossible smile of the day.

*

Afternoon is always busy with Rose.

At two months old, she usually eats her two bottles, burps, and then goes down till dinner; three hours of rest. But she seemed determined to stay awake during this lunch hour. It happens more and more as she finds her spirit and asserts herself.

Lucie went to the baby store for bibs only moments earlier, but not before warming up the bottles and placing them down with strict instructions: "Just these two," she said. "Don't overfeed her like last time."

I did as told—I gave Rose the two bottles of formula and one extra for good measure.

"Don't tell your mother," I said. Rose suckled until her eyes rolled into the back of her head, assuring me that our secret was safe. I hoped that the extra carbs might knock her out, but she remained on vigil, bright-eyed with a Caesar hair-cut, a little centurion on legionnaire watch.

When she doesn't go down, like today, we switch strategies and try to do tummy time for a few minutes so Rose can build her neck and back muscles. The exercise also tuckers her out most of the time. But even that wasn't working. Not equipped with any knowledge of babies whatsoever, I googled what to do when your baby refuses to sleep and up came this document about colic and burping properly. "Gas," it read, "causes great discomfort in newborns, leading to colic, which leads to crying. To avoid this, burp your baby regularly after meals. They sleep after."

Roger that.

I placed Rose on my knee, rubbed her back a couple of minutes, patted it a few more—I even have this rotation head maneuver Lucie always yells at me for, but it does get her to burp each time. I tried the wibble-wobble move, rocking her giant baby-head back and forth, front and back, and, to great satisfaction, out came the loudest belch ever—one like a grown man after a Mongolian feast; a compliment to the chef. A line of drool rolled down Rose's chin as she stared vacantly and caught her breath. A waft of milk perfumed my nose and grossed me out for a second.

Sour and warm, like raclette gone bad. I had to turn away to stop myself from vomiting. When I returned, Rose smiled right into my soul, drool now drenching her cherub cheeks. I couldn't help but smile back, the scent of nasty milk and bile still nauseating.

There goes another one, I said, a bloom upon my face.

★

I remember once watching a movie about an old lady living in a van. It was set in London and was a true story. Apparently, this lady had her van parked in the driveway of this writer fellow, and, as luck turns out, he wrote a play about her and it became this global hit and was made into this charming little movie. One of the most memorable lines in the film centred around love, or what love was, and the writer guy said, rather ticked off, "Love is shit, cleaning other's shit is love," or something of the sort. He was referring to having to pick up someone's feces—the old lady's, in fact. Her van obviously didn't have plumbing and whenever she'd use the bathroom, she'd shit in a grocery bag and miss the garbage pail on their property and create streaks on the trash can. He'd always had to pick up the bags over the years, wiping the rim when things got careless on her end. He did it, I think, because she was his friend, and, in a way, he loved her—exactly as he said. No other sane reason, really.

I never understood what he meant by "shit is love" until Rose was born this past November.

When we put her down during daytime hours, Rose sleeps pretty lightly in the family room crib. The creaks in the floorboards can wake her, same with Poppy Cat's pitter-patter on the way to the feed bowl. It's the cutest thing to hear Rose dream and wiggle about like a tiny glowworm underneath the blankie my mother-in-law Liba made for her. Sometimes Rose even snorts like a miniature swine rooting for truffles. And it's hard to tell from the recliner near the fireplace if she's just restless, if she's been awakened, if she is, in fact, a trained truffle piglet, or if she's dropping a load. I decided to go check it out.

Her face was turning blue when I picked her up. Her head darted around and she rumbled like a massage chair at the mall. Soft at first, then a crescendo of bowel gurgles that burst into a wet fart. A look of relief followed. My greatest fear, alone, and without the help of Lucie—the master of diaper disaster.

I panicked, utterly ill-equipped to handle such a scatolog-ical catastrophe, and chucked Rose down, forgetting to put the moisture barrier to catch any rogue liquids. I ripped off her diaper—again I forgot to put the emergency diaper underneath, rookie move—and saw waste smeared down her legs, up her bum, all over her back, through the blanket. She'd been marinating in it and was just giggling away.

It used to be that back before Rose was born, when some-thing went wrong as badly as this, I'd lose my cool and yell—typical male with a squirrel dick behaviour. But not today. Today I just looked at my daughter and she winked as I struggled with the diaper. I couldn't help but grin back—my *fourth* one of the day.

Turns out that writer was right—sometimes love *is* about shit, cleaning it for others, and doing it just because it needs to get done. Sometimes it's all we can do amid the chaos of life for our loved ones. The trick, as Rose's taught me, is to smile while doing it.

★

But that's what life is like now.

I collect my smiles. I keep my stars in my pocket. And I am happy.

I wrote the other half of my smiles down for that day, too. They appeared when Rose said what sounded like "hi" as we tuned into our nightly Jeopardy, how she clung to my chest like an Amazonian tree frog as I took her upstairs to bed, and when I stared into her face during her last feed.

This nightcap smile, my last of the day, was the deepest. I don't know—it is hard to describe—it's like my spirit was open. I had to fight back tears as Rose cooed and grasped the bottle. Lucie watched me, her eyes also wetter than a seasonal monsoon. We saw a cavalcade of expressions rush across Rose's face as she suckled. Newborn brains force their faces into all these different, and unrelated expressions, I think, for later when they'll match emotion and thoughts with their facial expressions. It's wild to see, and only happens in the first two months. They contort from angry to happy to upset to joyful and back to angry all in one or two seconds. In Rose, I saw a parade of current and past loved ones: my brothers, Josh, Jerry, and Daniel; my mother Blanche and father Sonny; my grandpas Jeremie and Cyril; my grandmothers Jackie and Nancy. I even saw further back in time, to my great-grandparents Myrtle the Turtle, David McKenzie, Samuel Thistle, Granny Whyte, and on and on. I looked over at Lucie in astonishment.

"Do you see this?"

"I do," Lucie whimpered. "I see my ancestors, too." We just stared for what felt like a million years, awed at the ancestral turnstile before us.

I realized then, smiling at my baby girl in the bassinet, that we'd won. We had, finally and completely, our own family. That Rose had brought us closer than we'd ever been in ten years of marriage. And that through her, our long-ago kin lived, somehow—the ones gone to the spirit world, and the ones watching over us. And it made me hope. A pure hope that one day, my descendants will look in my great-grandchild's face, long after we're both gone, and see Lucie and me staring right back, reminders that in the life of a newborn, we all get a chance to be someone's ancestor, even grumpy old men with long faces who forgot how to smile eons ago.

*

These next poems, as you might have guessed, focus around my domestic life now, with fatherhood and being a good husband and standing up and claiming my traditional roles taking centre stage. I start with moments in time during Lucie's pregnancy to capture the intimacy and the arduous, joyful journey it is. As the poems progress, I lift the reader's heart into the mother-and-baby unit at St. Joe's with Lucie's C-section performed by Dr. Luketic and her team, and then into our very home where we live with Rose today. Worry and love dominate this last section—ask any new parent and they'll likely describe similar feelings in the first few months. I also wanted to make this last section about my past nuclear family, the family I was raised with in Brampton. And, so, a few poems are about my grandpa Cyril, my brother, and how life has been since *From the Ashes*. In short, these closing poems are my most special, my most generative; what I would describe as the rays of starlight and love glinting off my shield's contours, crevasses, and characters. It's not very macho, I know, an ex-con writing a collection of pregnancy and baby poems, using your brain to create my images of child and family so they live forever in the public imagination, transforming them into immortal half-gods—but now they'll never die from Paris's arrow, quite unlike our hero of legend, and quite unlike me.

SWEET POTATO

My love's bump is now twenty weeks
still growing.
The pregnancy videos say
our tiny Elder is now the size of a sweet potato.

I don't know why I love that so much
but I do.

I read poems to her belly this morning
on the porch
over lattes
and we decided to play The Beatles' "Here Comes the Sun,"
to our coming daughter Rose's uterine ears
the purest thing we know.
Because all we need is love
and all love needs is us. Just as Paul, John, George, and
    Ringo told us, but in another song of course.

RUB

She's in her third trimester—only six weeks to go.
Achy legs,
up every two hours,
never-ending restlessness,
iron deficiency,
midnight snacks,
daytime snacks,
snacks upon snacks,
and swollen ankles.
She's looking for special shoes now
for when the baby comes, she can walk.
Just slip them on,
no fuss no muss.
But for now
it's pillows halfway up the wall,
props to hold her feet above her heart,
Netflix at night,
and foot rubs with special cream.

In the delivery room
she was stretched out on the operating table in a maternal
    crucifix.
There was this plastic shield covering her neck and chest—
it hid the theatre
the team of doctors rifling around in my love's abdomen.

"Never again," she said dryly, not impressed, as I took my
    spot beside her head.

She looked exhausted, the smell of raw blood and vaginal
    water thick and spilling onto the floor.

"Let's plan for a sibling," she said, changing her mind
    a second later, just as the doctor pulled our Rose from
    the wound, slapped her bum, and her cries coloured
    this world.

I saw Lucie's beautiful brown eyes well up. Then the
    layers of fat, her muscles sliced open, her deep reddish-
    black blood, the inside core of her uterus, the very
    inside of her soul.

She squeezed my hand. Even then strong and trying to
    comfort.

The anesthesiologist sprinkled some words across the beautiful carnage: "take it in now," he joked, "when I walk by my thirteen-year-old daughter's room she slams the door right in my face—and I don't even say anything!"

We giggled—such a terrible truth all we parents eventually know.

The surgeons laughed, too; Lucie's body rocked from the force. Clipping of scissors sounded out amid the blips of machines to keep her alive and awake during major surgery.

You know, I've seen lots of tough guys in my life. But never have I seen anyone or anything as tough as my wife that day in St. Joe's; a true gladiatrix.

The C-section line cut across her pubic hair.
Her body, fresh from surgery, was wheeled into this private
    suite only hours earlier.
It's hard to tell the trauma she's endured by her mood.
Amid hospital chow and me running to get "real" food,
she searches for her baby,
taken moments before by the doctor,
over and down the hallway
and across from the mother-and-baby unit.

It's 200 metres from Mommy's door to the NICU
where her child and other diabetic newborns or premies
are put on monitors
have tubes rammed into their little hands
and where nurses prick their heels
to check for sugar levels, to see who is hypoglycemic,
and who is deficient.

When I went home that night
she told me she might try to make the trek—
a yawning chasm, a distance I believed was impossible for her.
I said to rest.
That we could go over together in the morning.

I was surprised as anyone, when, at the crack of dawn, I had
	a text waiting:
a picture
of Mommy holding baby tight
the NICU nurses and incubators in the background, the
	neon lights all around.
I realized then
that nothing under heaven and stars
could've stopped her from seeing her baby—

not weakness
nor pain
nor being cut wide open by a team of surgeons.
Because she, Lucie, like all new mothers, is a powerful and
	unrelenting force of nature,
and she *was*—and *is*—the strongest woman in the world.

Salute to her.
And salute to every mother who has ever lived.

SOMEONE'S ANCESTOR

There is poo
fired right up her diaper
up her back.
How that happens—Creator only knows.

She cries every third hour
like a baby whale calling in the Pacific
some wolf cub spirit unrequited—
forever hungry,
forever searching,
forever thirsty.

The constant bending over into the bassinet,
the burrito wraps that hold her tiny but powerful arms,
the squiggles,
the milk spit up and bibs,
the pee—the surprise pee, a fireman's hose at midnight.
The blood-curdling screams upon first bath.

All of it is worth it—

to be someone's ancestor.

To see the generations across her face
through the life, the body, of this tiny little girl before me.
Born when the fall leaves were their most colourful,
born when the frost froze all the hate within me.
And born when everything else needed to die.

MINDFULNESS

Here we are
on the couch
on baby watch
listening to J. S. Bach's French Suite no. 2 in C minor,
writing trifles about early parenthood, fatherhood, love—
         present life—
scribbling down this very poem you're now a part of.

The stillness, between babe and poet and reader, is so blessed,
so precious,
so private.

It's not much, I know, but it's ours.

This fleeting moment in time, but a whisper floating upon
         the piano trills;
a story caught up in the gentle turn of my beat-up quill.

EPIPHANY

The baby howls at night.
First a whimper
then coos and a restless head
then piglet snorts—one wavy arm
then whines—body breaks free of burrito binding swaddle
then cobra hissing sound
then boiled tea kettle screams.

"Perhaps," I say, standing over her bassinet, "you cry so
    loud because you realize I'm your father."

I go in for a re-swaddle, but the cries continue on.
I know I would.

Her granddaughter's birth awakened her *Babička* superpower.
She'd been waiting years
for her little *kačenka* (tiny duck) to bob and wade life's waters
and to float into her arms.

Babi came to help the first week after the birth
like a shock commando storming Stalingrad
Tupperware containers like artillery shells
loaded with Czech comfort food.

Babi then bought half the baby store
a grey tornado of love and credit cards
and one-month-old jumpers galore.
It was a sight to see—a grandmother superhero with
    a perfect Equifax score.

And *Babi* toiled every night,
for three weeks straight
into the wee hours stitching *kačenka*'s blankie
and each knot was a chance back to herself
—a chance to clad her and her granddaughter's world anew.

HOLDING ON

I held on to
the greasy brown elevator overalls
the plastic radio
the old black wood stove
a rusty wire brush that survived the flood
and your favourite drill bit set,
the one you mixed with your woodworking bits; I held on
     to them as long as I could.

When I held them in my hands
I could still smell your cigarettes on those long-ago Sunday
     mornings
I could still hear your AM radio broadcasting out the garage
     and across our lawn
Hank Williams, Blue Jays' scores, and adverts ringing out.

I thought of you often since your death.
You came in especially strong when I held the belongings
     you left me,
the ones I've carted around hopelessly for ten years since
     they sold the old house.

When I first heard Lucie was pregnant
I finally got the courage to let go of your stuff—

to say goodbye
to grieve fully.

I threw out the brush first, then the overalls, then the drill
    bit set.
I felt somehow
that I needed to
make some sort of spiritual room
room in my heart
and room in my Earth
so your great-granddaughter could join us
so I could let go of you
so I could grab hold of her future and all the items she'll
    collect.

Only the potbelly stove remains; I just couldn't get rid
    of it too.
My dream is that one day the fire it carries will warm her
and give her something of real value to hold forever.
Just as when we cooked chestnuts upon its face
and you gave me love
and I first held on
back when I was just a little boy.

TWO BROTHERS

In the days
of wheat and beer
before the Nile ran red,
and the Temple Edfu protected our southern border,
Anpu and Bata, the ancient brothers
tilled the land.

Where once
they loved one another
the harvest of one
and the hardship of the other
caused the underworld to live
amongst their sun; caused the stars
to drown
in amongst the sea.

The rivalry bled.
The sands
the years
the eternal gulf widened
until care and goodness
was no more.
All replaced by war
desolation

and the sky cracked
and rained down stones.

Out of their eternal conflict
Anpu transformed into Anubis
and Bata into Horus.
The one the king of darkness
the other the lord of light
There, clutching their power
and never to love again.

This, the tale of two brothers.

A reworking of the oldest known writing in western literature, from the reign of Pharaoh Seti II 1200 to 1194 BCE.

Her left eye was closed when she was born.
And she rarely opened it.
Once in a while—maybe.

Goop crusted it shut,
and even when she smiled
the eye remained riveted.

Even with assurances from doctors and nurses, I worried.
I worried.
I worried all the same.

"But I guess that's what parenting is now,"
I told myself as I examined her eye and imagined the
    coming stomach ulcers parenthood was sure to give,
"I just hope it isn't lame."

TOOTSIE ROLL

She's my hard rock candy
she's got me wrapped like old-school hockey cards
this little piece of licorice made in heaven
this blessing of sugar.
I love how sweetness lays on her baby-back
flips onto her stomach
and does her tootsie roll move
and turns into the cutest piece of confectionary
in all of North America—
my sweet sweet baby girl.

BLACK BLOOD

The ancient spectre raises its head.
I awoke to my ankle scar black,
the flesh appeared necrotic.

The wax of rot gleaned
the deepest purple
where I had the bone trimmed years ago—my deepest yet
    most beautiful scar.

I imagined infection,
dead flesh,
and so lanced open the wound to make sure.

To my great surprise, underneath was alive and engorged
    with blood
—the black I saw.
The cold laser treatment I started recently is forcing blood
    into the scar tissue—some seventeen years after the fall.

Thank you, Dr. Stevenson, for trying something new, even
    as I resisted.

STEAM

At this hour
the morning sun cuts from the southeast
rays cascading upon the west-facing rooftops
that are blanketed with hoarfrost—white caps.

Mountains upon mountains, as that Arcade Fire song says.

There's a crispness in the winter air
this time of cleansing
the crucible needed for next year's growth.

I stare out the window
steam rises and dissipates off the neighbor's shingles;
water droplets dance toward sky, ever so,
freed finally
in the stillness of early January.

Epilogue

AD ASTRA

When I spoke at book clubs, which was quite often these last three years, I was usually asked how I survived such a bleak and desolate existence, a reality few in Canada know or have endured. I avoided telling them because I didn't ever want anyone getting too close to my heart. I had this weird superstition that if they knew about my shield it would lose its power to protect me—and I needed it amid the torrent of media attention and scrutiny brought by *From the Ashes*. Instead, I deflected and often told these book clubs that I was not unique; there are others like me—I know, because I've met them. They have similar stories of adversity and triumph far more dramatic than my own, and in many ways more important than my disability story—maybe they should be asked as well, I'd say.

Those other people who are both physically and mentally challenged, like myself, with limbs that don't respond, or survivors of horrific car crashes, or those who've fallen off buildings and crushed their wrists and ankles, or are hobbled mentally by something as awful as a missing person or parent in the family or a chemical imbalance; they all have, from what I know, some mental strategy to overcome their disabilities or situations in daily life. Some see themselves as operators of cool four-wheel all-terrain wheelchairs that conquer everything, even the largest snowbanks. Others pride themselves with that first step in the morning, legs wobbly underneath, the walk to the washroom as equal to an able-bodied person winning Olympic gold in decathlon. And still others disassociate and imagine themselves as anything other than their situation and current challenges, flying high above the violence of the Earth and their hobbled bodies and minds in a house where they are safe. People like us are incarcerated in our bodies in a way, but we manage to free ourselves by imagining a different future where we are limitless billionaires with the neatest gadgets, like Bruce Wayne; superheroes who have abilities beyond the pale of a normal corpus, cyborgs with titanium and scientifically superior limbs, and gods and goddesses who possess divine powers like wisdom, love, and kindness beyond what others can do.

Herein is why I focused on the most brutal and deepest scar I have—my Achilles tendon injury that both destroyed and rebirthed me into the person I eventually became. As I have shown, observing my scar revealed the beauty of my other scars, and truthfully, helped me stop feeling sorry for myself so I could try again—the scars became proof I had earned my tiny spot in the sun, that I had a right to live. The loss of my leg's function was totally devastating to me back then. The legend of Achilles, with his maligned foot and shield of poetry, was my way of disassociating and surviving, for to admit I was just a homeless crack addict with a severely deformed and infected foot that bordered on requiring amputation would have surely killed me. So, as cheesy as it is, I had to imagine myself as the fallen warrior of the ancient Trojan Wars; I drew on Achilles' strength and took it into my body, and over time it gave me the strength to first stand, then walk, and finally run. I mean that both physically and metaphorically—it helped me rehabilitate my body at Harvest House, and it helped me do superhuman things like go from functionally illiterate jailbird in 2009 to a published assistant professor in 2018. What makes it even more incredible, even to myself, is that I entered university in 2011 and was hired in 2018—just seven years later; and in that time, I wrote a book and countless other policy pieces and publications to help people where I once was. And I returned back home to my Métis-Cree family out west where I am, at last, an emplaced and loved community member—they say reconnection is decolonial. I don't know; I just wanted to see my mom.

I think my embodiment of Achilles, in the way I disassociated to tap into his god-like mental fortitude and stamina to achieve so much (more than I ever thought possible, that's for sure), was maybe why the legend was created by the ancient Greeks in the first place. My scar gave me an insight I don't think many people get: I've searched hundreds of classical peer-reviewed articles and none mention what I am about to tell you; I think, because they were written by academics, not by fallen warriors or veterans. Try to imagine what it would mean to an ancient warrior to be sliced across the back of their ankle and totally immobilized; their foot made useless; their potential to farm or fight or provide or even walk gone forever. And remember, this is the time of no social services or social welfare where people truly did believe in divine wrath upon the injured and would let you die in the street, military service or not. Their whole world would end, much like mine did, and for them there wasn't the benefit of things like antibiotics, safe surgery, or even proper aftercare. All they had was this legend of a fallen warrior who was once invincible.

One can look at the legend pessimistically and say Achilles died at Troy, was burned on the funeral pyre and turned to ashes (that was the hidden meaning of *From the Ashes* I never told anyone until right now), and then went to Hades as I did, or one can look at oneself optimistically and say, "Hey, I survived this horrific accident, where once this half-god did not." Do you know what kind of motivation it is to know you overcame something strong enough to kill a demi-god? And do you know what you can do when your scars become your fuel to fight another day? And do you know how powerful it is to have the god's shield to write your life anew in poetry, mistakes and all, your ugly and your beauty, your everything? Do you know how world-building that is? Well, take it from me: it is enough to bring one back into the circle from total dispossession, and by this, I mean with kin, emplaced in healthy social relationships in all avenues in your life; it is enough to find liberation and love, start a new family, and have a miracle baby in your forties. Again, as I've shown throughout this text, poetry literally created a new Indigenous life: my daughter Rose—there is nothing more generative than that. To that end, I hope my tiny book of poetry has shown you that it is possible, that we are allowed to imagine ourselves as something more, even if you're just some Métis guy with a broken heart living at the shelter with a rotten leg who thinks he's Achilles.

In closing, people often ask me how I survived to achieve such greatness (and by greatness I simply mean to be better than one was yesterday), and I have avoided sharing my shield until this very moment.

But this was how.

And now I gift you the fallen warrior's shield (even though you always had it), so you, too, can write your own poetry like I have done, and so you, too, can overcome and be who you are supposed to be.

Glory and honour to you, brave warrior.

Glory and honour to you.

ACKNOWLEDGEMENTS

I'd like to thank my daughter Rose. Your star shines and guides us forever home. You are our home—my whole life has been a journey to you—you've finally and completely given me belonging. Lucie, as always, you are my rock—everything good in my life stems from you. Thank you for leading me to poetry all those years ago. I love you; you free me; you are the light in my world. Next, I want to send a big shout out to my mother-in-law Liba who is the absolute coolest and most hardcore lady I have ever met—I wish I was a quarter as tough as your big toe. I cannot wait to smoke cigars with you and then marvel over the quality of your *langoše*.

I also want to thank my agent Sam at Transatlantic who made this little book of poems happen—her vision, along with Lucie's, was something I didn't see. Thank you for believing in our love poems, Sam; you're a total super-agent. We love you.

A big smoke signal goes to Jared Bland as well—the big cheese at McClelland & Stewart, who took a chance on my little shield of poetry. Jared, like Sam, knew the power of this collection and created a path to publication. Jared organized the original legion of poems into nests and then wrestled with me, back and forth, and through some brutal edits I did, until we had a coherent narrative of meditations. I still marvel at how you steered me to write—like a conductor or matador (I know both are cliché but so very true for our work relationship).

I would also like to thank the folks at M&S, managing editor Kimberlee Kemp, copy editor Terrence Abrahams, and graphic designer Emma Dolan, for your editorial mastery and keen design-eye. I really was blessed with the best, kindest, sharpest-eyed on this project.

Finally, I would like to thank my paternal blood cousin Karen McBride who did the illustrations. Your powers were what was needed to lay medicine over these scars and so they could heal, finally. They are so beautiful and were the perfect addition to this book. I chose you because you are related through my Grandmother Jackie McKenzie's family in Timiskaming and I wanted to honour her Algonquin-Scot people, whom I haven't really written about yet, and so I chose one of her kinfolk. I knew I wanted to have you illustrate since that time in Vancouver when we learned we were cousins.

In closing, I am astonished how this team—all mentioned here—allowed for such creative expression and made this book of old poems happen. The depth of writing really shows this fearless process. May you all treasure it as I do, and hopefully Rose will in twenty years.

Marcee.

ABOUT THE AUTHOR

JESSE THISTLE is Métis-Cree, from Prince Albert, Saskatchewan, and an assistant professor in Humanities at York University in Toronto. *From the Ashes* was the top-selling Canadian book in 2020, the winner of the Kobo Emerging Writer Prize for Nonfiction, Indigenous Voices Award, and High Plains Book Award, and also a finalist for CBC Canada Reads. Jesse won a Governor General's Academic Medal in 2016, and is a 2016 Pierre Elliot Trudeau Foundation Scholar and a 2016 Vanier Scholar. A frequent keynote speaker, he lives in Hamilton, Ontario, with his wife, Lucie, and is at work on multiple projects, including his next book. Visit him at JesseThistle.com.